Happy Place

**Ten Simple Guides to Finding
Calm, Relaxation, and Tranquility
through Your Inner Self**

§

Sayed Ahmed

Order this book online at www.trafford.com
or email orders@trafford.com

Most Trafford titles are also available at major online book retailers.

Printed in the United States of America.

ISBN: 978-1-4269-9791-4 (sc)
ISBN: 978-1-4269-9792-1 (e)

Library of Congress Control Number: 2013905292

Trafford rev. 03/20/2013

North America & international
toll-free: 1 888 232 4444 (USA & Canada)
phone: 250 383 6864 ♦ fax: 812 355 4082

Smile more often, love yourself, love everyone around you, and live life to the fullest.

CONTENTS

INTRODUCTION

The Realization

As I sat down to eat lunch, I couldn't help overhearing two well-dressed people telling each other about their stressful situations—how life was getting complicated and filling up with obligations. One of them said to the other, "I'm stressed. If only I could leave everything."

Suddenly, it hit me: It doesn't matter if you're rich or poor, young or old—we all face stress and want to find a place to retreat, to find a sense of calm and tranquility. I wanted to find out what was preoccupying people and causing stress in their lives.

I started to do research online and began reading books and looking at my life experience. I discovered that we are avoiding the little things in life that we can be grateful for, like picking a flower. Laughter is literally the best medicine. Positive thinking is the best tool.

Therefore, with my experience working with people and my educational background in biology, the study of life, I began to compile research, believing in my ability to find the ultimate guide to help me overcome stress. I started to put together this to-the-point book, which I feel people can relate to. I know that having a "happy place" can help people find a sense of calm when life becomes too overwhelming. I hope you find and enjoy your happy place.

Sayed Ahmed, 2011

CHAPTER 1

What is a "Happy Place"?

As human beings[,] we all want to be happy and free from misery. We have learned that the key to happiness is inner peace. The greatest obstacles to inner peace are disturbing emotions such as anger and attachment, fear and suspicion, while love and compassion and a sense of universal responsibility are the sources of peace and happiness.

—Dalai Lama

What is a "happy place? Happy place is the mental state achieved when a person wants to avoid unpleasant surroundings. Everyone's happy place is different, and usually consists of the things that will make them happy. Makes sense. But if we were to ask thousands of psychologists and sociologists to define it, they would give us thousands of different answers. So let's simplify it.

We are too often extremely busy and have too much on our minds. Almost every day, we have to deal with stressful situations, pressure, unexpected circumstances, obstacles, and obligations at work, home, or in the outside world. Therefore, we often think of going someplace to escape, a place to release our tension, a place that will help us have a sense of calm.

We may call this our "happy place." A happy place can help you get through the many negative situations life throws at you. It can help you cope with stress, physical illness, and loss of mental energy. Having to deal with these issues can lower a person's self-esteem and ultimately make a person less social. Many psychologists and sociologists believe that when a person is overwhelmed with stress, going to a happy place may help restore a healthy balance in one's life and allow him or her to work things out. People who have a happy place will have mental stability, an oasis, ultimately helping them take back their lives.

But the question is, how do we balance our lives and get to our happy place when everything around us becomes unhappy? Let's take it systematically. Everyone is different from one another; therefore, everyone's happy place will be different. Some of us will consider having a new car, a better job, or more money a happy place. Some will make religion a happy place; some will make family, friends, and relationships a happy place; and some will make just being healthier a happy place. Whatever it is, we all just want to escape from our daily stressful lives and restore our sense of balance—in the simplest way possible.

Things we think will take us to our happy place:

- Financial security
- Winning the lottery
- Family/loved ones
- Spouse/relationship
- Success in life
- Religion/faith
- New house
- New car
- Vacation

Right now, you are possibly thinking, *Okay, I know everyone is stressed, and how important it is to escape to a happy place. But how do I get there when everything around me is preventing me from going to that place?*

The first step is to think of stress as a natural feeling. While a little stress or pressure will keep you on your toes, anything extra will cause harm. With enough practice, we can overcome obstacles and difficult circumstances, but it all comes down to us as individuals.

What is stress?

Now let's look at it more in detail. Stress is a normal physical response where you feel your life is unbalanced, where an event makes you feel threatened or sad. When you sense danger, your body's defenses go into high alert quickly and an automatic process known as the "stress response" kicks in.

The stress response is the body's way of protecting you. When you deal with stress properly, it can help you stay alert, energetic, and focused. Stress can help you tackle a presentation at work; it sharpens your attitude to help you win a game; and it gives you the extra energy to study for an exam when you'd rather be with your friends.

But when too much stress occurs, beyond a certain point, stress stops being helpful and starts causing major problems with your mental state, your health, your productivity, your relationships, and your quality of life. Stress can come about anytime, without your knowing, and that's when you get used to it, thinking it's normal to feel it. Without your noticing, it affects your life, taking a heavy toll on you, so it is important to realize when stress levels are out of control and know the signs and symptoms of too much stress. Stress affects the mind, body, and mood in many ways, and everyone experiences stress differently.

Top eleven signs and symptoms of too much stress

1. Memory problems
2. Unable to concentrate
3. Constant worrying
4. Moodiness
5. Short temper
6. Feeling overwhelmed
7. Loss of intimate relationship
8. Increased heartbeat
9. Eating less or more
10. Isolating yourself from others
11. Nervousness increases

It is important to know that not all stress symptoms are detectable. If you believe that you are experiencing too much stress, seek help from a doctor.

Things that help you decrease stress level

- A support team—It helps to have a strong, supportive network of friends and family members in a difficult situation.
- Your outlook and attitude on life—Many people have an optimistic view. They embrace challenges, have a strong sense of humor, accept that change is a part of life, and believe in a higher power or purpose.

- Dealing with your emotions properly—You're extremely prone to stress if you don't know how to calm and relax yourself when you're feeling emotional. The ability to bring your emotions into balance helps you bounce back with a sense of control.
- Your knowledge, wisdom, and preparation—The more you educate yourself, the more prepared you will be about any stressful situation, including how long it will last and what to expect. It is like a coping mechanism. For example, if you know you have a big exam, you should study or ask for help. The more you study, the easier it will be for you, thereby reducing your stress level.
- Your sense of control—If you have confidence in yourself and your ability to find a way to get through challenges, it's easier to take on stress and move forward.

Let's face it: with all the problems going on around us, like job loss, relationship problems, debt, and financial problems, why wouldn't we feel stressed out? And that's only part of what many of us go through on a daily basis.

Top five reasons we have too much stress

1. Financial problems
2. Relationship problems

3. Job issues
4. Life-changing events
5. Being too busy

Your actions and decisions will determine the outcome. Think about what is making you stressed and mentally preoccupied. Identify the problem. Is it a relationship, unemployment, money problems, or unexpected circumstances?

Whatever it is, think about what will make you have peace of mind and stop thinking about all the stress life throws at you. Sometimes you'll have to stop and phase out everything around you to get to your happy place. Okay, we know that not everyone is able to do this. This may take more time or be more difficult for some. The point is that we want to make it easier to get to that happy place.

With enough practice, a person can have a sense of calm and tranquility if dealing with stress positively. Let's say you have a project to do at work. You get a call from your boss, letting you know that instead of ten days to do it, it now has to be done in four. You are understandably stressed, and you think you can't do it. Suddenly, you have a positive idea: you can ask your coworkers to help finish your project. Positive thinking is a strong energy that will bring you closer to what you want.

As we are aware, stress can have many different causes, such as family problems, relationships, job issues, financial problems, poor health, emotional breakdowns, or even the chronic illness of someone we know. It is very important to find the causes and then take time to deal with the root of the problem in order to simplify the situation. Always remember that while we don't pick the situations that come to us, we can choose how to deal with them.

Nirvana—freedom from pain and worries

What is "nirvana"? In some Asian cultures, nirvana is associated with one's happy place. It is a place of freedom from our pain, worries, and the external world. But how to attain nirvana?

First, we must accept that stress and the circumstances causing it are not avoidable, like aging or death. We must each pick our path from all the stress and suffering. The main suffering comes from ignorance, envy, and anger.

Second, we should search for a way of life that makes us able to grow spiritually. We should be on a constant journey of self-knowledge. Our thought process should be free of the three poisons: envy, anger, and ignorance. We must do all of our jobs and daily works with morality.

Third, we must learn to calm our minds using meditation, to find peace of spirit, and not to become overwhelmed with every little problem.

Ask for help

Pride should not get in your way, because this is one of the best sources of support. Don't hold your stress and frustration in; this will only make things more complicated. Think about what is making this more stressful and separate that first. Some stress comes along without our noticing, and if possible, we should take steps to deal with the core of the problem or ask for help from friends or loved ones. In some cultures, people go to their elders for guidance and solutions. If it gets worse, seek counseling.

Scenario

Mike has been married to his wife for four years, and they have a daughter together, but they are constantly fighting. Mike is getting fed up, and so is his wife. What should Mike do?

Mike thought about leaving, getting away from all his drama at home, and even getting a divorce. But Mike also thought about his daughter (Mike's happy place), and he talked to his wife about putting their differences aside. They decided to go to marriage counseling and talk things out.

Do you have a happy place?

Have you found a place where you can go to in your mind or to any other quiet place to reduce stress and relax? What place will help you retreat? Is it thinking about the birth of your child or your wedding day? Is it time spent with your friends or family on vacation?

Stress always comes our way, and it sometimes can lead to serious illness and emotional breakdowns. We may feel tired, frustrated, depressed, or ill—and possibly even feel as if we are losing a sense of control over ourselves. In fact, stress is known to increase the chance of getting an illness by over 90 percent. A happy place is a place in our minds where we can get away from all the problems and relax or meditate to release stress when life gets too overwhelming. Many of us just want to have calm and relaxation. Here are a few ideas to help you find your own happy place:

Guide 1: How to get to your happy place

1. Find a place where you can relax

Be comfortable and find a place where you can relax your mind and your body—a place where you are alone and away from the stressful situation or negativity. It could be a peaceful place like a park bench, your bathtub, on a beach next to the sea, or any location where you have happy memories or enjoy spending time.

2. Concentrate on your breathing

You should close your eyes and focus on your breathing. Don't breathe too fast. Breathe slowly and deeply in through your nose, hold it for a few seconds, and then exhale through your mouth. Push all the bad and stressful thoughts out of your head and just concentrate on your breathing. Breathing in oxygenates the blood, sending red blood cells in our brains, making us calm and relaxed. When we breathe too fast, it makes us anything but calm. For example, when we are angry, we breathe out too much carbon dioxide from our blood, which results in panic attacks, sweating, faintness, and dizziness, resulting in hypertension.

3. Think of your happy place

As you continue breathing slowly, bring back memories from your memory lane. Think about a place where you would feel truly happy. Imagine yourself with friends or family. Think back to when you were younger and went to the basketball court or to the roller skating rink with your friends. Think about a vacation you took, a trip to a museum, or walking in the park or garden.

4. Focus deeply and relax

Focus deeply on your happy place. Concentrate on your senses, the smells and sounds, and the feeling that is happening. Now you should feel your body starting to relax.

Take advantage of all of your senses. Your senses will help you reveal many happy thoughts and situations. Your senses will allow you to have an overwhelming sensation of happiness.

5. Stay there for a while

Keep your thoughts on where your happy place is and you will get in a calm and relaxed state, allowing you to return refreshed and renewed.

You need to be willing and have the desire to take some time for yourself for ten to fifteen minutes, to unwind and leave your stress behind.

Now, whenever you are overwhelmed with stress, you will be able to go to your happy place and have a sense of calm.

CHAPTER 2

Take Action/You Are in Control

The critical ingredient is getting off your butt and doing something. It's as simple as that. A lot of people have ideas, but there are few who decide to do something about them now. Not tomorrow. Not next week. But today. The true entrepreneur is a doer, not a dreamer.

—Nolan Bushnell

Now that we have identified the roots of our stress, it will be easier to go to our happy place. Stress does not discriminate due to your religion, your income, or your race. Remember, stress happens to everyone.

It all depends on individual actions. Your actions will determine the outcome of any situation.

This is your life. Take control of your life and all your plans. Never let any obstruction take control of you. Make your plans ready. Your goals will only become realistic based on your actions. Tell yourself that it's now or never!

One thing you should always remember is that the world and everything in it is always changing, and things change quickly. It's like technology: you have a new phone, and then the next month the next version of the phone is released. So have all your hopes, desires, and goals ready, especially the things that will change. Make your plans accomplishable; don't make them too difficult. Start one step at a time. If you want a relationship with someone, approach the person and be open and honest. See if that person wants it to. If not, just move on. It may be hard, but you will know the truth. If you want to overcome a conflict with someone, you can be the bigger person and start the conversation. Talk it out and if feelings are still hurt, you may need to give it time. Eventually, it's going to work out.

Let's look at it this way: we all get too much stress and unwanted circumstances. The key is to make it simple and address them accordingly. One of the main stresses comes from financial problem such as rent, paying bills, or getting out of debt. Do you or anyone you know rely on chance and luck to win the lottery, or do you hope that money is just going to come along? It's normal to have dreams and think you will win or money will come along, but don't lose sight of reality. The chance of someone winning the lottery is extremely low. You have to be realistic and take action instead of waiting; if you want to have more money, do something about it. Try to be more effective. Look for more options, which you will always have, to get a better job, open a business, or invest your money.

The simplest way to get out of a financial problem

The simplest way to get out of a financial problem is to budget your spending and save enough cash to pay any surprise bills. A budget is a financial plan that specifies a specific amount of money to be spent on certain commodities like food, clothing, rent, entertainment, and savings. Here's how to use a budget to reduce your financial problems:

- Know how much you are making every month.
- Figure out your fixed expenses, such as bills, food, rent, and clothing, and separate them from your non-fixed expenses, such as movie tickets, nights out, and other forms of entertainment. Carefully record your monthly spending.
- Stick to your budget.
- Now that you can see what your expenses are, eliminate any unnecessary items.

- Make a list of all of your monthly debts. Pay off the debt with the highest amount of interest first, while continuing to pay at least the minimum monthly payment on your other debts.

If the financial problem persists, another way to reduce your debt load is to borrow money. But don't borrow so much money that you can't pay off. Borrow enough to get back on track. Then you can pay it off with your present income.

If it gets worse, seek counseling. Go to a professional who can help a chronic debtor come up with a manageable budget and develop a debt management plan.

Helpful tip: Not all counseling is legitimate. Some firms charge hidden fees. Find one you can trust.

Have a plan and write it down

It's simple—write down what you want done. How many time have you forgotten to do a task or goal? For some, it happens quite often. Many more tasks and goals are completed and achieved when you write them down. In addition to writing down everything you want, be sure to indicate how you plan to get what you want. Perhaps one of your goals is to have more money. To accomplish this, decide whether you need to go back to school or if you should train to get a better career.

The more action you take toward what you want, the closer you will be to achieving your goals. Of course, things don't always go according to plan, and you probably won't achieve everything all at once, but never give up. Keep on going. You will definitely make great progress when you follow your list of plans.

Again, writing your goals down is a good technique. Since we live in a mobile society, almost everyone has a handheld device. Take advantage of that resource. You can type your list on your cell phone and take it with you when you travel. In addition to writing down your goals, you can write down positive thoughts as well and take the list wherever you go. If you feel down, just refer to what you've written down.

Let your mind be open and free. Not all your writing has to be done at once. You can write whenever it is convenient for you.

Guide 2: Write it down

1. Set some time

You should set some time where you won't be disturbed to be peace at mind and be able to write. One of the best ideas is to make a list of things you enjoy and make you happy: people, hobbies, foods, music, activities, and so forth. Be as open as you can with this list; try to use everything from low to high happy thoughts.

2. Write positively

Write down as many positive memories that you can think of. If you have difficulty or run out thoughts, here is a great tool. You can say, "Remember that time . . ." or "Remember when . . ." This will definitely make you remember happy memories.

3. What are you grateful for?

Begin a page of what you're grateful for. We as people often forget the little things in life. It could be as simple as walking, picking up a spoon, or smelling a flower. We don't think of these things, but the reality is that when we think deep down, we will have hundreds, even thousands, of things that we can be thankful for in our lives.

If you want to make this a continuous process, another good writing technique is having a personal journal. Include in it all your happy thoughts for your happy place. You can use this journal day after day, but always be consistent. Keep your journal close to you, cherish it, and you may discover many unrevealed secrets you thought were lost but were there all the time, waiting to be uncovered.

Now you can take the next step, making a "bucket list." This is a list of things you want accomplish before you get older or pass away. You may want to travel the world. You may want to find yourself in a life journey, accept nature rather than material goods, or you may want to do something better for yourself or your loved ones.

As we know, stress is too often a problem for many people. It is difficult to do other things when stress occurs. Here are some ways to release stress when you need a pick-me-up or are on the go.

Exercise

- Find out why you are stressed.
- Seek a quiet place to relax.
- Find anything that will make you happy, like pictures, your religious items, and so on.
- Get a small box with a cover.
- Put your items in the box.
- Keep the box in a safe place and within easy access.
- If you become stressed, get the box and sit in a quite place where you won't be disturbed.

This a good exercise even if you are at work or traveling. You can take the box with you.

Take control: This is your life

To overcome stress and unexpected circumstances, you have to take control of your life. Always remember that this is your life and you have to take control, even if life becomes too overwhelming. You will always have options.

We have to realize that life is too short to live our lives too fast or be stressed. We must come to an understanding of all that life has to offer. Don't rush—take your time. You cannot live life like a fast car taking the expressway. Slow down and the take the slower path. By taking the fast lane, we tend to miss all that wonderful scenery, the little things in life, and the opportunities that life has to offer.

Guide 3: Take control

1. Think positively

If you think positively, you will attract positive things and they will ultimately happen. So feel positive and have a positive mental attitude. Positive talking gives an extra boost and energy for taking on each day.

If you want to accomplish a goal or task, you can start by passionately saying the following: "I can do it" or "I have to get it" at least five times in a row. For example: "I can do it, I can do it, I can do it, I can do it, I can do it." See the difference it makes.

Helpful tip: A therapeutic trick is to walk around with a rubber band around your wrist; as you notice negative self-talk, pull the band away from your skin and let it snap back. It will hurt a little.

2. Let your emotions out

We as people believe that our emotion should be expressed in the appropriate manner at the appropriate time. But sometimes this may not always be possible.

Learning to deal with your emotions is extremely important. Sometimes you need to let your emotions out, but you still want to stay in control. We can make our emotions work for us or get us down. When we experience happiness, we feel as if we can take on any task. On the other hand, if we experience sadness, a simple task can seem too big.

Don't let your anger get the best of you. Control your temper. In most cases, anger will cause you to make irrational decisions that may not be in your best interest. So try to get over it as soon as possible. Turn your frown upside down and smile!

Like Yoda, a character from the movie *Star Wars*, said, "Anger leads to hate. Hate leads to suffering." This could also be said also for envy and envy.

Many of us hold our feelings and our emotions inside. This is like putting too much helium in a balloon, waiting for it to pop at the wrong moment. Eventually, your feelings and emotions will explode, hurting you or someone you know. We have to come to the realization that it is okay to feel the way we feel. Don't be afraid of reactions from others when you express you feelings. Yes, telling someone the truth may hurt, and other times, people just won't understand. But holding your feelings in too long will create problems and cause resentments. Now, when you try to express your feelings, you might be frustrated or in a bad mood, potentially turning a conversation into an argument. Instead, open a conversation by saying "I am feeling . . ." Don't feel bad about you emotions and feelings; what you feel is part of being human.

Get some alone time and let your emotions out. If you need a good cry, watch a sad movie and let it out; if you want to laugh, watch a comedy. This is a good cleansing technique for your mind and emotions. Let it out and get back on track. Stress can also create other emotional reactions such as frustration and anxiety. It is important to listen to positive and relaxing music or watch movies that can help you go to your happy place.

Have a support person you know is going to listen to your feelings, someone you can call when you are feeling down. Better yet, have a support group. Your support group can meet up once a week to talk about each others' feelings and sorrows. Find people you know will support you and be sure to support them as well.

3. A Plan

You have to set a goal for what you want to achieve today, not tomorrow. Remember, plan your day and stick to your plan. Jot down a to-do list. When doing this, be as realistic and specific as possible about what you can accomplish each day.

Do not try to do too much. We often forget to consider our limitations and squeeze in too many tasks in one day. Know your limits and do not push yourself too hard or beat yourself up when you do not accomplish all your goals.

Do the most difficult and unpleasant task first, getting it out of the way. Do not procrastinate; that only puts more stress on you. Finish each task in a timely manner. Never let your tasks become a project; then they will be difficult finish.

Sample to-do list:

6:30 a.m.	Wake up
7 a.m.	Exercise
7:30 a.m.	Make a healthy breakfast and make sure kids are up
8:00 a.m.	Send kids off to school and go to work
9 a.m.-4 p.m.	Work, taking a ten-minute breathing and stretching break as well as a lunch break
5 p.m.	Shop for household necessities: food, detergent, and so forth
6 p.m.	Healthy dinner for family or mix it up and go out
7:30 p.m.	Do some household cleaning
8 p.m.	Help kids with homework
9 p.m.	Relax

The point is to be as realistic and specific as possible, allowing for flexibility. For instance, if you want to change it up, go out to dinner occasionally instead of always having dinner at home.

4. Schedule and organize your day

When you schedule your day, include some relaxation time, as this can reduce the amount of stress you must deal with at any one time. Add some breathing techniques (see chapter 1) and stretching space to allow you time for recharging and creative thinking. This will help you be better prepared when an unexpected task arrives. At the end of the day, review your goals. When you are finished with today's tasks, relax and prepare tomorrow's to-do list.

Helpful tip: When stress and tension come along, take a deep breath through your nose and release slowly through your mouth. This will release some negative energy.

Much of our stress comes from being overwhelmed, resulting from lack of organization. Get a planner. Always be organized. Being organized can help you break responsibilities down into less difficult tasks and focus on the things that really matter.

Many of us wake up every morning looking at our lives and feeling overwhelmed by so many things to do. The carpet hasn't been vacuumed, the kids' toys and clothes are all over the house, and dinner hasn't been made. Using a planner can make your life much more organized. Organize each day so you can accomplish each of your tasks and projects, and gradually this will become a habit.

We cannot change everything

If something can't be changed, don't be disappointed or beat yourself up. Learning to accept things as they are is important. It is a coping tool. Some things in life are out of our control. For example, suppose you have an ill grandmother who raised you and now you are caring for her. You know she is going to leave you soon. It's sad, but it's time to just accept the situation and be with her.

Take responsibility for making your own life. No one is going to come with a silver platter and hand you your life. It is going to be difficult to make decisions and take action on them. However, it is much better than feeling powerless and reacting to decisions made by others. Decide what you want and then go for it.

Take control of your diet, mind, and exercise

We've all heard that the most important meal of the day is breakfast. So start your day with a healthy breakfast or a healthy snack. You need to treat your body right; otherwise, where else will you live? You will have more self-confidence and energy, and you will be physically healthier. Take control of your diet, physical activity, and bad habits.

Your choice of food is important when you want to start a positive day. A dietician will tell you to stay away from sugary and salty snacks and have fruits and natural foods instead. Be smart and eat right, knowing which vitamins reduce stress and which foods contain vitamins to help you control your diet.

What is a healthy breakfast?

Many cereals provide multiple nutrients, but look for those that are high in fiber as well. Fiber helps your digestive system and lowers your overall cholesterol levels. Consider using skim milk rather than whole milk in your cereal.

A bowl of oatmeal each morning is healthy for you. It will help lower your cholesterol and reduce your chances of heart disease. If you don't like oatmeal, try a fruit and yogurt parfait. Eat more fruits overall. Also eat nonfat yogurt, antioxidant fruits, and low-fat granola made with healthy grains such as oats and bran.

If you are like some people, you want to eat a traditional breakfast like bacon and eggs, and you can. Just be sure to make what is typically a fatty and high-sodium breakfast healthy. For example, eggs are a good source of protein, but the yolks also contain a lot of cholesterol. We can separate the yolk from the egg and eat the egg whites. Bacon and sausage taste great with eggs, but eat turkey sausage and bacon rather than the traditional pork or beef, which contains high levels of saturated fat, cholesterol, and sodium. You will want to make the healthier choices at lunch and dinner as well.

Guide 4: Diet/exercise/meditation

1. You are what you eat

Start the day with a glass of water and continue to drink water throughout the day. An average person should drink a minimum of two liters of water a day and have a limited amount of sugary carbonated drinks, which will add more stress. Water is the best beverage, as it flushes out all the toxins from our bodies, making our brains sharp and energized.

Many of us rely on coffee to wake us up and keep us going, but too much caffeine is known to raise stress levels. Coffee contains caffeine, which stimulates your senses, waking you up and increasing focus. But too much caffeine can harm you. Not only does it raise stress, but it also increases nervousness and restlessness. So limit your intake of regular coffee and caffeinated beverages, finding a natural solution instead. In fact, according to research, apples are great at helping us stay awake and energized. So consider substituting an apple for a cup of coffee.

Granted, with so many greasy, fatty fast-food temptations like burgers and fries, we may tend to eat these items more often than others. But eat smart and be healthy. Eat proportionate amounts, including less high-calorie food and lots of raw fruits and vegetables, especially greens. This is the best way to stay healthy.

Have a healthy balance of eating food and control your diet. A good way to do this is to have a healthy snack before a big meal. This prevents us from eating more than we should. You can follow this eating habit:

- Healthy breakfast
- Healthy pre-lunch snack
- Healthy lunch
- Healthy pre-dinner snack
- Healthy dinner

Helpful tip: Keep on hand more fruits and healthy snacks, instead of sugary high-calorie snacks, at home or when you travel. This will help you make a habit of eating healthier.

Yes, natural, organic food is more expensive, but you will definitely benefit in the end. Keep in mind that you are investing in yourself and your well-being. Your body will feel refreshed and energized when you eat healthy snacks such as fruits and nuts. Uncooked and unprocessed fruits and vegetables have more vitamins and nutrients. Eating raw, whole foods can lead to weight loss, more energy, and even allow people to avoid illness. Your health is literally in your hands.

You can eat chocolate. According to studies, chocolate releases endorphins, a chemical in our bodies that helps combat pain and lower stress levels. It also contains healthy antioxidants and flavonoids. Eat chocolate in small amounts, however, and opt for dark chocolate when possible.

Eat a banana. You probably aren't aware that eating a banana can make you happier. Bananas contain potassium to relax you, vitamin C for vitality, and vitamin B6 to help combat stress. They also produce serotonin, which helps prevent depression. So if you are feeling a bit low or lacking in energy, have a banana. Bananas are also helpful if you want to lose weight, as they are filling and can satisfy your need for something sweet. Many athletes frequently eat fruit, mostly bananas, as they are a good source of energy.

Vitamins and minerals

Remember, before self-medicating, it is important that you consult your doctor. I recommend taking vitamins and minerals; some vitamins can help you deal with stress:

- Vitamin A—Antioxidants in this vitamin help alleviate stress, giving an individual a more effective stress-coping mechanism. Foods containing vitamin A include milk, liver, butter, eggs, and fruit.

- Vitamin B complex—This is perhaps the most important of the stress-relief vitamins and minerals, working on several different parts of the body to provide anxiety-reducing mechanisms. Niacin, one of the B complex vitamins, is responsible for maintaining metabolism, which is necessary for the creation of serotonin, which is a neurotransmitter promoting a stable and balanced mind. Niacin can be found in peas, beans, meat, poultry, fish, and grain-based cereal.
- Vitamin C—Vitamin C is responsible for the creation and maintenance of the hormone cortisol, which has an important role in stress levels. Also, vitamin C provides effective stress-coping mechanisms due to its antioxidants. Vitamin C can be found in oranges, grapefruit, lemons, limes, tomatoes, berries, cabbage, lettuce, and peas. Foods containing vitamin C should be eaten raw so the positive effects will not be lost.
- Vitamin E—Vitamin E acts as an antioxidant in the body. Although the effect of this vitamin on stress is yet to be fully understood, it is thought that it has properties that alleviate stress. Vitamin E is found in nuts, cabbage, lettuce, and certain types of oils.

2. Exercise

You don't have to be a bodybuilder—just exercise at least a little every day. Stay fit. Even ten to fifteen minutes of exercise will make a difference. Exercising will make you healthier and improve your physical appearance, giving you healthier skin and a better body shape.

Psychologists tend to agree that exercise provides a dependable way of releasing tension and stress. Exercising helps us have better posture, making us stand or sit up straight instead of slouching, which results in increased confidence levels. As the saying goes, "Keep your head up and be strong." This has numerous psychological and physical meanings. But one of the main ones is that when we stand up straight and keep our heads up, we feel more confident about tackling any situation.

Exercising helps you sleep better. It increases the body's temperature, which relaxes the muscles, inducing a feeling of calm and tranquility. Exercising also releases endorphins, the chemicals in our bodies that relieve stress.

Do a minimum of five minutes of stretching exercises. Stretching will allow you to relax both your mind and body.

3. Get enough sleep

Getting regular sleep is one of the most important habits. The average person should have at least six to eight hours of sleep every night. If you don't have the average amount of sleep, it affects every area of your life, including your health, stamina, relationships, and even your career. The quality of your sleep also affects the decisions you make and your ability to handle life's problems.

For those of who can't go to sleep easily, there could be a variety of reason. We may have to replace the mattress, release some emotions before coming to bed, or alleviate outside distractions. In some cases, it could be caused by medical reasons, like insomnia. There are myriad ways to overcome difficulty sleeping, including massage therapy and sleeping aids. If insomnia becomes serious, seek professional help.

Wake up early and start the day. Doing so will give you an extra boost to tackle the day. You will be surprised how many things you can accomplish.

4. Positive self-talk

Say something positive to yourself as soon as you get up. Starting the day on a positive note will allow you to be in control and set a goal for what needs to be achieved. Many psychologists and researchers think that one good way to start a positive day is to have a good self-talk. This is one of the best tools you can use to face things positively and go to your happy place.

You can overcome many negative situations by saying one or both of these phrases: "I can take on this task, one step at a time" or "Since I've dealt with this before, there's no reason why I can't do it now." When you know that you are going to face a stressful situation, rehearse how you are going to handle it.

5. Mental videotape

Picture yourself overcoming it successfully. Create a mental memory that you can play repeatedly in your mind. In other words, visualize your stress. Have a mental scene and, if needed, play it over and over.

6. Laughter is the best medicine

Laughter is literally good for you. Laugh a little or, better yet, a lot. Laughter puts a person in a better mood. Laughter increases disease-fighting interferon protein gamma-n and increases T cells and B cells, which make disease-fighting antibodies. This benefits anyone suffering from diabetes, as it lowers blood sugar and relaxes the body. It also speeds recovery after surgery. Having a sense of humor about a situation is a great tool; it's okay to step back from the seriousness and see the humor in a situation.

7. Don't keep it bottled up

Again, many of us keep things bottled up, and we should avoid making this a habit. Talking to someone can be extremely therapeutic. If you keep things bottled up, it can only cause more stress, and you will feel irritable. Communicate your feelings. Telling others you need help can only improve the situation. By opening a line of communicating, you are also creating a path for a solution.

8. Meditate and do yoga

Learn to meditate and let the stress go. What is mediation? It basically allows you to get in control of your mind and have positive thoughts and emotions. And when unpleasant thoughts come to mind, you will be able get rid of them.

Exercise

How to meditate

- Find a quiet place where you won't be disturbed for at least ten to fifteen minutes.
- Sit down, relax, and rest your hands on your lap.
- Sit on the floor cross-legged with the support of a cushion, or you can sit on a chair with your feet resting on the ground. It's not necessary to force yourself into a lotus position if you're not used to it.

- Maintain the natural curve of your back. That means no slouching. People with back problem who can't sit for long periods can find other sitting positions.
- The next step is breathing slowly and deeply. Close your eyes softly. Begin by taking a few slow and deep breaths: inhaling with your nose and exhaling from your mouth. Don't force your breathing. Let it come naturally. You should begin to feel calmer and more relaxed. That means it's working.
- Now focus your attention on your breathing. Be aware of each breath that you take in through your nose. Cancel out everything else and think happy thoughts.
- Finally, when you are ready to finish, open your eyes and stand up slowly. Stretch and then proceed to focus on your activities.

Do yoga. The word yoga means "union," and it was practiced in India thousands of years ago. We can think of the union happening between the mind, body, and spirit.

Yoga refers to the practice of physical postures or poses, a system of education for the body, mind, and spirit. Yoga can also be a good stretching technique for your body. Go to you to the library or video store and get any copy of yoga for beginners; you will learn numerous yoga poses. Follow it and you will be one step closer to calm relaxation.

Get some alone time and take a bath; this will give you time to be calm and relax your body. You can take this time to think positive thoughts. Don't fall asleep.

Again, stress is one of many problems we deal with, whether it is caused by work, family life, friends, drama in a relationship, or money problems. But your actions will depend on ways of relieving it or distressing it. Don't ever think that it's hopeless. Don't ever give up.

If you are too overwhelmed, you may want to drop everything. You may want to throw all your "baggage" away and just relax for a few minutes or even a couple of days. Take this time and go for a short walk to clear you mind. You will not resolve any issues if you have too much on your mind. If that doesn't work, go on a short vacation and you will come back rejuvenated, perhaps even feeling that you have left the stress behind. Even just lying down on a bed with your eyes closed for a few minutes can help. Try to let your mind go blank.

CHAPTER 3

Alternative View: Religion/Spirituality

This is my simple religion. There is no need for temples; no need for complicated philosophy. Our own brain, our own heart is our temple; the philosophy is kindness.

—Dalai Lama

Faith is believing in what we cannot see.

As we know, this is a sensitive topic. In the dictionary, we find the following: "Religion is of mind or way of life expressing love and trust in God, and one's will and effort to act according to the will of God, especially within a monastic order or community; as, he achieved *religion*." Some people think religion will bring them closer to their happy place. Is this the case? It is sometimes said that religious people are happier than nonreligious people are. If so, why might this be?

Some people believe that they have a higher purpose in life. Some people came to a realization and accepted that while our lives are important, there is a bigger force than us in this universe. Throughout history, many people believed that life is empty without religious faith. They believed that God's love was blissful in the afterlife, and that there would be paradise. Researchers and psychologists all around the world have been intrigued by these beliefs. Many studies have simply asked people how happy they are, although studies differentiated from people to people. Considering some of the experiences people have had in their mosques, churches, or synagogues are vastly different from the kinds of experiences that researchers studied and investigated.

According to a 2010 study by Harvard researchers published in the journal *American Sociological Review*, researchers found that people who went to church regularly reported increased levels of happiness over those who didn't. The critical factor was the social aspect and the quality of friendships made in church. Researchers also discovered that when people who didn't have any outside support or outside friends attended religious services, they often made close friends and were more satisfied with their lives. The research shows that having friendships based on mutual interests and meeting consistently based on religious beliefs makes a lot of difference.

Researchers also asked why they are happier. These are the top three reasons why religious and spiritual people are happier.

Top three reasons religion brings happiness

1. The social support and sense of identity. People are generally happier when they are around others who are supportive, and out of this comes a social connection that can be helpful and supportive in many ways. This is a positive sense of belonging we all seem to look for in our lives.

People in religious groups share one another's burden, reach out to those in need, and offer friendship and companionship. Statistics show that the majority of people who attend religious services are single people, the elderly, and those in poor health, for they are often looking for support. Religion also helps people feel support from God, who might be viewed as the ultimate supporter.

2. Sense of direction. Religion brings happiness and life satisfaction in a time of need. It increases the sense of where we are going and what is important in life. Religion helps us better understand the meaning of life. Religion offers a sense of control over one's life and purpose. Religion and faith can help a person understand that an unexpected event, like traumatic illness or unexpected death, is usually out of our control. Religion offers spiritual growth in order to handle these situations.

3. Their relationship with God. Religion gives people a sense of hope. God is a sense of refuge for people in times of trouble, offering the idea that there is a loving, caring God to whom you can go for guidance. Religion offers the belief in living life simply. Considering that there is a blissful afterlife is comforting to people. Religion offers a person a feeling of being in contact with a higher being (God) when needed. Religion offers unconditional love, and people have a sense of security from God.

For many people, these are usually considered positive things, and of course, if someone is more involved in positive things, he will tend to feel happier than someone who is less involved. A person's relationship with God can be a source of comfort in troubled times.

Religious experience leads to a happy place

Religious experiences may lead to long-lasting increases in a person's happiness, which will take him to his happy place. Religious people often follow their hearts and souls when making decisions. They are more connected with God, whom they seek as the ultimate happiness, which is the sense of belonging and unconditional love.

On the other hand, some studies also show that there are occasions where some religious environments are associated with people being less happy. For example, if friends have a conflict over religion, the pain can be deep and long lasting. Some religious conflicts are much bigger than conflicts with friends—like families against families, or even cultures against cultures. And then there are people who go to extremes in the name of religion.

But the majority of people have a sense of certainty that they will be with like-minded people and find a sense of support. Clearly this is a topic where many questions and answers remain to be uncovered.

Keep an open mind

Some of you might be thinking, *What if I don't have a religious or spiritual bone in my body?* That doesn't mean that we can't be open-minded about research on finding a happy place, even if it's through religion. Many psychologists are suggesting that religious people are happier, healthier, and recover from illnesses faster than nonreligious people do. Consider three examples:

- Research shows that a greater number of people who report attending religious services describe themselves as happy and having a sense of direction.

- Statistics show that if someone ill undergoes a serious surgery and is comforted and receives strength from religion and faith, he will be likely to recover three times faster.
- People who go to religious services have a sense of support. They believe they can open and express their feelings.

Power of Prayer

The practice of prayer is one the most spiritual practices in the world. Many people pray on a regular basis and attend religious institutions as well, feeling more connected to their happy place with prayer. Praying can be done anywhere, at any time.

But can anyone say a prayer—and can it make us happier? The answer to both is yes. For instance, you can address every prayer to happiness, joy, support, and the connection with God. For example, consider this one by Robert Louis Stevenson, a Scottish novelist and poet who lived from 1850 to 1894. His best-known books include *Treasure Island* and *The Strange Case of Dr Jekyll and Mr. Hyde*.

> *Grant to us, O Lord, the royalty of inward happiness, and the serenity which comes from living close to thee. Daily renew in us the sense*

of joy, and let the eternal spirit of the Father dwell in our souls and bodies, filling every corner of our hearts with light and grace; so that, bearing about with the infection of good courage, we may be diffusers of life, and may meet all ills and cross accidents with gallant and high-hearted happiness, giving thee thanks always for all things.

Religion and spirituality do have a great impact on people who want to find a sense of belonging. For some, religion and spirituality are the same. For others, spirituality is about a journey of seeking wisdom, striving for personal growth, and searching for meanings. Most people need to feel that they matter, that their suffering and hard work will count for something, and that their lives have a purpose. They need to feel a sense of control over their fates. We have to open our hearts and accept it. But keep in mind that religion is not founded on scientific experiments or analytical reasoning. It is founded on acceptance of personal growth and wanting to find a purpose for our being, especially in situations where we want to find answers to the questions that science can't analyze.

Nonbelievers can go to religious services

Throughout the world, nonreligious people have tried to see what it must be like to go to religious services or participate in religious activities. Almost all of them have found the same results: social and emotional support from one another, values, people finding more about whom they are, people having a better understanding of their meaning in life, comfort, and relief from stress. Most important of all, they found hope—a reason to say, "I can do this." They gained a sense of control and strength to deal with challenges and much more.

Can nonreligious people who don't want to be affiliated with any religious services do something like this once a week? Yes, they can. They can get together with like-minded people and listen to each other and talk with one another about something greater than themselves, like helping people who are suffering or in need of help. People are experimenting any way they can to find a sense of support.

We may look at the great story of Gautama Buddha. Gautama Buddha was a South Asian spiritual leader who was born in Lumbini, a town in modern Nepal, near the Indian border. He lived between approximately 563 BCE and 483 BCE. Gautama Buddha was born a prince; he was destined to be a king.

During the birth celebrations, a prophecy was announced that this baby would become either a great king or a great holy man. Gautama was isolated from religious teachings or knowledge of any human suffering. Although his father ensured that Gautama was provided with everything he could ever want or need, Gautama was constantly troubled internally and spiritually.

At the age of thirteen, Gautama was escorted by his attendant to visits outside of the palace. There, he came across the "four sights": an old crippled man, a diseased man, a decaying corpse, and finally an ascetic. After that, Gautama realized the harsh truth of life: it is not all luxury, but death, disease, age, and pain. He learned that the poor outnumbered the wealthy, and that even the pleasures of the rich eventually end. Gautama was inspired and left his home, his life of luxury, and his family at age twenty-nine. He chose to become a monk. He left his inheritance and dedicated his life to learning how to overcome suffering. He took on the path of Yogic meditation with two Brahmin hermits. At the age of thirty-five, he attained enlightenment under the full moon in May. He was then known as Gautama Buddha, or simply "the Buddha," which means "the awakened one."

The Buddha made it clear that he was not a God but that the position of Buddhahood is reserved for a human. The Buddha is solely a guide and teacher for those who are seeing the path themselves, who want to attain spiritual awakening and see truth and reality as it is. The Buddhist system of insight, thought, and meditation practice was not divinely revealed, but rather, the understanding of the true nature of the human mind, which could be discovered by anyone for himself. He emphasized the truth: that ignorance can be eliminated.

For the next forty-five years of his life, he traveled the Gangetic Plain of central India (region of the Ganges/Ganga river and its tributaries), teaching his experience and discipline to all ranges of people, from nobles to street sweepers to outcasts. His teaching was open to all races and classes and had no caste structure.

Just before his passing, he was admitted to the Sangha (Buddhist order), and immediately after, Gautama passed away on a full moon day in May. The Buddha's final words were, "All things must pass away. Strive for your own salvation with diligence."

Religious environment have a great impact

Religious people who go to church, mosque, or temple tend to be closer to their happy place. Even though we take into consideration that every person is different—and factor in personal income, health, education, number of friends, activities, and so forth—research shows that people who go to religious places and belong to religious organizations find better understanding of life and are closer to their happy place.

Sometimes it depends on how religious your surroundings are. The more religious your surroundings, the happier believers are. If your surrounding is not as religious, then nonbelievers are happier than believers.

Whether we are Muslim, Christian, Hindu, Jewish, or atheist, we should all agree that as long as we are together with like-minded people, we a have a sense of support and comfort and can go to our happy place. We are responsible for our happy place. We can't always blame life and circumstances for our depression and hopelessness. True happiness is not determined by the events, circumstances, or relationships in our life.

Go to your neighborhood mosque, church, temple, or synagogue and see if you are around like-minded people. See if you can relate to them.

A body without a soul is empty

What is a body without the soul? Just as with our physical bodies, we need to take care of our souls. We should always nourish our souls with positive and inspirational material. Different people are inspired differently; some are inspired by reading religious quotations or inspirational quotes by famous people, others by reading such religious holy books as the Quran or the bibl. Some get inspired by biographies of successful people. Whatever it is that inspires you, do it. This is good nourishment for the soul.

This will give you the ability to make positive changes in your attitude, which generally helps you make better choices. Fill your life with confidence and be determined to achieve your hopes, dreams, and aspirations more spiritually.

Gratitude

Be grateful. When we really think about it, there are a million things to be grateful for and to be happy about. We should stop whining and complaining, for it is not going to make a difference in our lives. It will only drain our energy and keep us from doing things that will improve our lives. Instead of saying "Why this?" or "Why that?" or "It always happen to me," you can say, "This happened to me once, and now I can teach others not to do it." If we list all the things we can be grateful for, our moods will change immediately.

People that feel grateful experience less stress and anxiety, resulting in a sense of calm. They enjoy more vitality and optimism. If you can't find any things to be grateful for, you can be grateful for the simple things that we sometimes take for granted, like breathing air, drinking water, feeling the sun that makes life possible, and so on.

"We as people look at the big picture all the time, but sometimes we have to look at the small picture. Otherwise, we will go insane."

Gratitude is essentially being thankful toward people. It is one of the most important feelings, for it brings joy and happiness to our hearts. Every time you are feeling anxious or stressed, stop everything you are doing right away, take a deep breath, and remember all the people in your life—or even those people you don't know but who are helping you, such as those we remember with gratitude who died defending our freedom and who died for humanity.

Life is neutral. It never picks sides. We as people have opinions and decisions about what happens. Circumstances that may seem to be "bad" for you can turn out to be opportunities for somebody else, so try to recognize yourself as part of something greater than yourself. You learn to be at peace with your life when you don't worry too much.

As they say, "Worrying is like a rocking chair; it takes a lot of energy and doesn't get you anywhere."

CHAPTER 4

Overcoming Obstacles/From Obstacles to Opportunity

The only fool greater than the one who expects big results from small changes is the fool who believes big changes can be accomplished without risk. Opportunity and security are inversely proportionate; as one goes up, the other goes down. It's a fundamental law of the universe.

—Roy H. Williams

We have so many obstacles and challenges to overcome in life. Some obstacles can be easy to overcome, but some are not. There will always be circumstances; this is where making smart decisions comes in—taking action as far as what needs to be done.

To overcome obstacles, we should know the difference between making right and wrong decision. You should always say, "This is my life, and I am in control. Many things will try to stop me, but I have to keep on going." Knowing right from wrong can make a big difference in overcoming any obstacles. There are things in life that can seriously negatively affect you, but there many things that are not that bad. Whatever obstacle comes, you have to make a good and bad decision, but the best decision always comes from your heart.

Think back to how many opportunities you could have seized. Remember this: life gives you opportunities. When an opportunity comes, you have to take it. There is a big difference in saying that you might do it and actually taking action. So resolve to pay attention and get back on track.

Helpful tip: When the overwhelming feeling of being in difficult situations outweighs the effort of changing them, accept the challenges with courage.

Make your own path and share your own experiences. Write a book, be a photographer, be an entertainer (DJ, singer, or dancer), or open a business. See what you are passionate about and do it. Believe in yourself; create the urgency. If you procrastinate, you may lose your momentum.

Become one with the challenge

We will always have challenges in our lives. But remember that in order to overcome challenges, we have to become one with them. This will get you through tough times and get you good results. We all have natural God-given physical, psychological, and spiritual tools. If you make use of these tools, you will be able to accept any challenge with courage and enthusiasm, and soon you will make effective progress. Some challenges are there to help you reach your goals—to give the extra boost or to keep on your feet.

For example, some of us have a friend or relative who is disabled, whether blind, deaf, or physically handicapped. But people's disabilities do not stop them from living life. Yes, they have huge obstacles, but this does not stop them from going to the supermarket or the park. And many of them accomplish their goals.

Consider, for instance, people who are in the Special Olympics. These people tended to live lives of neglect and isolation, excluded from social events or participating in school. They transformed themselves as athletes, participating in challenging games, which others thought impossible.

The only thing we have to fear is fear itself

Let's discuss the words of Franklin Delano Roosevelt, the thirty-second president of the United States: "The only thing we have to fear is fear itself." Don't be afraid of challenges or obstacles; instead, we should embrace them. You are the victor, not the victim. Victims always complain, while the victors find solutions. If you are faced with a challenge, don't focus on the problem more than you need to. Yes, many situations can be extreme and frustrating, but it is important to remember not to get stuck because of negative feelings.

You may need to cry or scream aloud until you release that negative energy. Then you can move on. If you sit there keeping hold of your negative feelings, you will be making things worse than they have to be. You will feel better with your life when you embrace challenges rather than resisting them.

Mind over matter

Living well should be a mind-set, not a process. Freedom of our minds is the most important tool we have. We can control and are responsible for what we think about and how we think about it. Let your mind be free.

This does not mean we are responsible for every obstacle that comes along the way. Many challenging obstacles are beyond our control; this is when the universe comes into play. It does not pick sides or listen to our human needs and wants. Believe in the universe.

Believe that the universe is fair and neutral, and we are all connected. When the universe is good to you, it is good to everyone else. Vice versa, when it is bad to you, it's bad to everyone else. You may not see it at times, but trust it and you'll be amazed. Every event is connected. Nothing is separate. Everything is part of a perfect order that the universe knows, but we can't understand it with our separate minds. It also works like a ripple effect. We only see the little parts of the universe at work, and we judge them as being "good" or being "bad." Remember, the universe is neutral; it is at work for everyone.

Become grateful for the negative forces (see chapter 3). This changes focus. What's the right approach for overcoming obstacles? We don't know. It depends on the individual person.

Guide 5: The right approach to overcoming obstacles

Here is a guide that will help us tackle obstacles with better focus.

1. Acknowledge the obstacles

Say to yourself you have an obstacle

2. Acknowledge how you are feeling

Once you have done that, identify the real feelings. Ask yourself, "How am I feeling right now? What emotion am I feeling?" Sometimes it isn't easy to figure it out. When you have figured it out, laugh aloud and say, "It's anger, stress, anxiety . . ." Don't hold it in.

3. Be aware of how you talk

Keep this in mind when talking to your inner self. Start with positive self-talk.

4. Be aware of negative phrases

You might catch yourself thinking things like this: *Why does this always happen to me?* and *I'm never going to get this right.* When you do, laugh and say, "There it is!" Identifying it means that you are on the road to recovery.

5. Replace negative phrases by being specific

For example, use "this time" or "in this particular instance" or "it just happened that time." You could say, for instance, "It happened to me that time, but next time I'll know what to do."

6. When you feel you are to blame, laugh

Then say, "There it is!" Then find some way to remove the blame or just replace it with happiness. Make it fun: "My coworker received the employee of the month this month, but I'll get it next month."

Question your inner self

One of the critical steps is to ask yourself, "How do I want to feel better right now?" Answering yourself with some positive thoughts and feelings can actually make you feel better. If you can't manage it directly, at least think of something else that will make you smile, some experience you've had or a funny situation that happened in your past.

As the saying goes, "It takes one brick to build a house." It takes one small step to begin any big journey. When you see your progress slowing or you get stuck, it's important to know how to get unstuck. It may be a simple solution or support. Over time, progress always comes with any obstacle. When that time comes, commend yourself. Keep hold of that feeling as long as you can, letting your frustration become happiness and your grin turn into a big smile. You will be surprised to see how things will change for the better. Hold it for a few more seconds and then get back to anticipating your next action. Tell yourself that something good will happen soon. Expect it to happen. This will transform a losing attitude into a winning attitude. This will turn your attitude, your life, and your focus around. Don't try to figure out why it works. Just do it.

Subconscious level

Now let's focus our attention on the subconscious level. This is where dreams happen. This is where many negative and emotional unresolved issues are hidden. It is like storage for all your life memories. It is also where we can imagine all the things we want to get every day. With enough practice, we can program our subconscious minds for happiness and remove all the negative limiting beliefs.

First think of positive thoughts. Then you can also feed your subconscious mind these thoughts: thoughts of accomplishments, love, good health, and enjoyment. You can start each day programming your subconscious mind to show you the positive qualities that you have. With enough practice, you can develop any positive quality you wish. The more you practice positive behaviors, the more you will become confident.

As we know, happiness is a state of mind. Sometimes we subconsciously think of negative thoughts. But we have the power to overcome any problem that occurs. Realize that your subconscious can solve many problems.

True happiness will come into your life the day you realize that you can overcome any problem. Timothy Walter, or "Tim Burton," an American film director, film producer, writer, and artist who is famous for such movies as *Charlie and the Chocolate Factory* and *Alice in Wonderland* says, "I've always been more comfortable making my decisions from the subconscious level, or more emotionally, because I find it is more truthful to me. Intellectually, I don't think like that because I get uncomfortable. I'm more wary of my intellectual mind, of becoming delusional if I think of it too much."

Like one's soul, the subconscious has to be enriched with positive thoughts.

The teaching of Zen

We should also look at the teaching of Zen. Zen is a way of life in Japan, and it began in China, where it was called Chan. Zen is the Japanese name for Chan, a school of Buddhism that was transmitted from China to Japan in the twelfth and thirteenth centuries CE, and it became very popular in Japan. Chan had become the most dominant Buddhist school in China. Japanese Buddhist monks traveled to China to study and returned to establish Zen in Japan.

Zen focus clears up the mental space and energy to produce results. Zen teaches that the enemy of focus is distraction. Distractions are like a pack of wild wolfs. Distractions are small, fast, and fierce, entering our lives and threatening to eat up our most precious resources: time and attention. Learn to concentrate your energy and stay focused.

Here are some guidelines for attaining Zen

- **Distractions:** Be honest and open. Know what things are draining your time and energy. List them, acknowledge them, and separate yourself from them.
- **He said/she said:** Don't waste any energy on gossiping and talking negatively of others, friends, family. Focus on your life and the positive.

- **Have human contact:** We are in a time where we socialize through the Internet or social media. It's good to have connection through social media when friends and family are otherwise not within reach, but try to maximize speaking to your friends or family face-to-face.
- **Positive mind-set:** By focusing on positive thought, you bring in positive energy. This brings in people who get things done, people who encourage happiness and will help overcome difficult times.

Keeping your mind clear of negative thoughts and stressful distractions helps you live a Zen lifestyle, focused on passivity, purpose, and peace of mind.

CHAPTER 5

Courage/Changing Your Life

We immediately become more effective when we decide to change ourselves rather than asking things to change for us.

—Stephen Covey

Many people are unsatisfied with their lives. Are you one of them? Do you often think, *If I knew then what I know now* . . . or, *If only I could start fresh and be the new person I can be* . . . ? Do you want to start fresh? Do you often think, *If I could only have a remote to rewind my life* . . . ?

If yes to any of the above, that means you want to change and make your life better, whether financially, emotionally, or with a relationship. To do this, you have to accept change and be willing to change. Yes, you need to change in order for you to make your life better. Change is inevitable, which means it will happen and can't be stopped, like aging. You will not be able to get to your happy place if you don't realize you cannot stay the way you are, making you stuck. You can't grow if you don't change the way you think and act.

In fact, changing your life for the better is an ongoing process. It never ends. The moment you stop changing, you stop growing, but you must know how to start. As we know, the most difficult part of change is always the beginning. Once you go through with it, things will become easier. You have to maintain the momentum. For example, think about pushing a car. The most difficult part is getting the car to start moving. Once it's moving, pushing it will be easy as long as you don't let it stop again. Similarly, you should keep improving your life. Change your life day by day. No one knows everything about life. Everyone is still learning. But here are some things we can share:

Guide 6: Accepting change

1. Be willing to change
What differentiates us from all the other animals in the world is the power of will. Being willing is vital. This is your life; no one can change it but you. If you are not

willing to change, then nothing in this world can make you do so.

To build your willingness to change, first you have to come to a realization that your life can be better than it is now. Even if your life is good, it can always be better physically, emotionally, or spiritually. Keep this in mind; don't feel hopeless if your life doesn't seem good right now. Have courage and you can always change your life for the better.

2. Slow down

To change your life, you need to take some time to think and reflect. If you are always busy, you won't have the time to think about your life and take action to change it. So slow down and make room for change. Slow down and enjoy life. You don't only miss the images going by too fast; you also miss the sense of where you are going and why.

As the saying goes, "Stop and smell the roses." This widely used phrase means to take time to appreciate a situation or to slow down and pay attention to what is going on around you. It is also commonly used when talking to someone who seems too busy to enjoy life.

3. Accept your responsibilities

Accepting responsibility for your life is crucial. We as people often blame other people for every bad thing that happens in our lives, like our families, friends, bosses, or the economy. Stop and accept it; whether your life goes up or down depends on you. Once you take the responsibility, real progress will happen.

4. Find your deepest values

Look deep down in your heart. There are some values that you know are good and true. We all have some values instilled in our hearts. Take some time to find them. See what you are good at. What do you think the most valuable thing in your life is? Do you have principles you can follow to live a fulfilling life? For example, you might want to volunteer. Align yourself with these values. Find them and remind yourself every day about them.

Do you have a reason to go forward?

Every one of us needs a reason to get up and go forward; this is also called our "cause." Like success, this is one of main keys to change. Just as a car needs a powerful engine to go, you also need a powerful source of energy to overcome the things that get in your way. You need the passion and the ambition to change.

Your cause is the source of energy you need. Your cause can give you the strength and courage to make you change. If you don't have a cause, find it. No one can give you your cause. To find your cause in life, find what matters to you most. For instance, we go to work to have shelter and food. Our cause would be having shelter and food for ourselves and our loved ones.

Still, change is not always easy, for there are may be emotions and habits you need to overcome.

Your habits

We all have good or bad habits, and we need to identify them and list them. We have to realize that our habits have a big impact on our lives and change process. Identify your bad habits and then replace them with good habits. Some bad habits slow us down. We need to find them and replace them.

Instead of wasting so much time and energy on breaking our bad habits, we should focus on creating new good habits that will replace them. For example, let's say that your bad habit is watching too much TV. Rather than focusing on reducing your TV time, you should focus on building a positive habit that will use your time in a better way. For instance, you might want to make a habit of going for a walk.

One good habit you can have is starting your tasks with the intention of finishing them, and with the right expectations, you will be able to do so. Otherwise, you will be disappointed easily when things don't go as expected. It is important to know that change takes time, especially if you want the change to last.

Having the right expectations will prepare you in difficult times. Suppose you want to go on a vacation from work two months from now. Know that unexpected things might happen—staff might be short or your vacation date may change—and prepare yourself.

Life is not always about finding yourself; sometimes it is about creating yourself."

You can replace bad habits

Think about it like this: If you could pick a couple of your bad habits to replace in the next few months, habits that will have the most impact on your life, what would they be? This isn't an easy question. Many of us often ask ourselves this question, but we get nervous when it comes to starting positive life changes, which is natural.

There are so many bad habits we might have to replace, from quitting smoking to sleeping in late to spending too much money . . . and many more. And all are important life-changing habits. But if we were to start again and had to pick one or two, what would we choose? Remember, change doesn't happen overnight; it may take a few weeks or months. You have to commit and stay focused.

> *Men's natures are alike; it is their habits*
> *that separate them.*
> —Confucius

Exercise

Creating a new habit is not easy. But the only way to develop new habits is starting from the beginning. Here are the basics:

- Notice a bad habit.
- Write it down on paper, along with your motivations, obstacles, and strategies for overcoming it.
- Have a person you can rely on when you see yourself slowing down or getting stuck. That person can then give you a push.
- Most important: You have to commit fully. Hold yourself accountable and track your progress day by day.
- Commend yourself for every little success.
- If you fail, figure out what went wrong, plan for it, and try again.

Okay, now you will be able to change a bad habit to a good habit. But remember to only make one change at a time.

Like cause, your belief system is important

Not everyone is aware that we have two types of belief systems: limiting and empowering beliefs. The words tell it all. Limiting beliefs are beliefs that limit you, and this is the system prevents you from changing your life. You need to find them before you can effectively handle them. To find your limiting beliefs, think about the thoughts you have that contain words like *I can't* and *I won't be able to*. Whenever you find one, write it down. After some time, look at your list. These are the beliefs that are limiting your ability to change.

After figuring out your limiting beliefs, you need to replace them with empowering beliefs—beliefs that encourage you. Write positive statements to replace the negative one, and make positive affirmations using those statements.

Do it whenever you realize that a negative belief is at work. For example, instead of saying, "I can't ride the bike," you can say, "With enough practice, I will ride this bike." It is important to write it down.

Again, positive thinking is one the most important habits that will help you create other good habits. Positive thinking certainly goes a long way to motivate you to do the other things you may need to do to be successful.

It may be as simple as changing your daily routine

Most of us have felt at one time or another that our daily routines are just more of the same. It can often feel as if your life is a hamster wheel, running in a circle. You get up, brush your teeth, get ready, head off to work, come home and do chores, make dinner, help the kids with their homework, and go to sleep, only to get up the next day and do it all again, right? Well, the truth is, life can certainly feel this way at times. How can we change this?

It's simple: mixing up your daily routine can make a big difference in your life. The best routines come at the start and end of the day. Develop a routine for when you awake, for when you first start working, for when you finish your workday, and for the end of your evening. For example, do something completely different and unexpected. Take the family to a movie or get up early and make their favorite breakfast. Doing something unexpected will break up your daily routine and will likely catch your family off guard, giving them a chance to loosen up and enjoy themselves.

How will that change your life? Most importantly, it may help you connect with them in a better way. Further, if you are doing something new in the morning, it can boost your day; if you do something different in the evening, it will help you burn off the stress and tension of the day.

Eventually, you'll be adding new ideas for change to your daily routine, and it won't feel quite so much like a hamster wheel anymore. You will be able to focus on what's important, not just what comes up. It'll help you make sure you get all your tasks done every day. And that can mean a lot.

Kindness is a habit

Some may not know this, but kindness is a habit. It's like our "mojo." And the more pleasant you are, the more good will follow. Focus on it every day for a month and you'll see many changes in your life. You'll feel better about yourself as a person. You'll see people react to you differently, and they'll treat you better.

It's like karma. Karma means "a distinctive aura, atmosphere, or feeling." Someone might say, "There's bad karma around the house today. Basically, karma means that every cause will have an effect, that what goes around comes around. Every good you do will come back as good; every bad you do will come back to haunt you.

Guide 7: Making kindness a habit

1. At the beginning of the day, make a goal to do something kind for someone on a daily basis. It could be as simple as helping the elderly cross the street or giving up your seat to a pregnant woman.
2. Each time you talk to someone, try to be kind and friendly, be lenient, forgive, and soften your attitude.
3. If you want to go beyond kindness and do a compassionate act, volunteer to help those in need.

Helpful tip: Kindness is not weakness if it's expressed with wisdom. Kindness can be a strength if you help someone who is in need, but some people can take advantage of it and try to manipulate you.

Multitasking leads to overwhelming stress

Contrary to popular belief, multitasking does lead to stress. Many of us have too much on our plates, which leads to multitasking. Our jobs or personal lives can lead us to multitask, but we are more effective and efficient when doing one task at a time. It's hard to achieve important things if you're constantly switching tasks and distracted by other important things. If you single task, you will be less stressed and happier throughout the day.

Although it may difficult to do, if you focus on one goal at a time, it is the most powerful way of achieving your goals. When you take on many goals at once, you spread two critical components, focus and energy, thin.

"But what if I have more than one goal I want to achieve?" you may be asking. You should first pick one goal to focus on. Break that goal into smaller goals that you can accomplish in a set period, such as a week. It's okay if it takes longer, but finish it. Pick an action you can do today. Keep doing this until the goal is accomplished. Do an action every day. Finish the first small goal and move on to the next small goal. When your finish your first complete goal, focus on the next goal, also breaking it into smaller goals if necessary.

Some goals are ongoing ones, like studying or exercising every day. In those cases, you can turn them into habits. Focus your thoughts on turning the goals into habits until the habits are imbedded within you. Then focus on the next goal.

It is crucial to set your priorities and identify the important from the unimportant things in your life. Then eliminate anything else that is complicating your life, like people, bills, or relationships. This will definitely simplify things and leave you with the space to focus on the important things. This process will work with anything—with life, work, tasks, and communication. This will change your life because it will help you to simplify, to focus on what's important, and to build the life you want.

> *We first make our habits, and then our habits make us.*
>
> —John Dryden

CHAPTER 6

Learn to Love Yourself

Love yourself first and everything else falls into line. You really have to love yourself to get anything done in this world.

—Lucille Ball

You've probably heard people say that you can't truly love someone else until you learn to love yourself. Do you believe in this statement? If you do, you should be your favorite person. When you come to this realization, it is amazing how everything around you can change. Like the importance of developing relationships with others, it also makes sense to improve the love of yourself first since you are with yourself all the time.

It's going to take a lot of effort, commitment, will—and it requires changes in your mentality—but there are several ways you can learn to really love yourself. One thing is certain: if you don't set your priorities, starting with yourself, no one else is going to do it for you. It's true that you can be your own worst critic and destroy your self-confidence more than anyone else can.

The average person has three thousand thoughts a day. Why not make most of them happy thoughts? When you start to have a negative thought about yourself, stop and replace it with something positive. It is going to take some effort; you'll have to change your mentality and change some habits you've likely had for a while (see chapter 5). However, the more you do it, the easier it will be to start thinking of the positive rather than the negative.

For example: This will help you to talk to someone whom you have a disagreement with, when you feel like something to say to the person, and you feel, it is going to come out negative, replace it in a way that will start a conversation rather than arguing.

Enjoy the positive and delete the negative. Be happy; don't be a grouch.

Get back up and try again

If you make a mistake or fail at something, get back up and do it again. Don't beat yourself up or talk down to yourself. Think it as a learning experience.

Let's look at Thomas Alva Edison, an American inventor. He was credited for the invention of the lightbulb. Thomas Edison failed many times, and each time he failed, he made notes of what he'd done wrong in detail. Then he made adjustments and tried again. He learned all the components, discovered all the chemicals and elements that wouldn't work. But he thought to himself that each time it didn't work, it was a step closer.

It is said that it took Thomas Edison more than ten thousand experiments to invent the perfect electric lightbulb. Considering that this was the first time a lightbulb was invented, he couldn't go look it up in a book or use other references. He simply had to fail and learn during the process, until his invention worked.

Stay in a positive environment

People who are educated, well established, loving, and have positive experiences typically give off positive vibes and positive energy. If you are around negative people, it can have a great influence on your mood, which, in turn, can affect other areas of your life. If you are in a positive environment, it ultimately brings you up. It only makes sense to be around positive people.

We definitely need to address the negative people in our lives, and if they can't change, then we should let go of these negative influences. Try to separate yourself from anyone who brings you down. It may not be easy, especially if you consider yourself close to those people, but you need to surround yourself with those who make you happy and bring positive energy and thoughts into your life. As much as it hurts to let go of certain people, you will later find that being happy with yourself is much more rewarding than being surrounded by negativity.

Signs of being around positive people

- You feel safe, relaxed, and want to get closer.
- They put out good vibes, have good hearts, and are compassionate and supportive.
- The have peaceful vibes.
- You feel your energy and level of optimism increase.

Signs of being around negative people

- You initially feel unsafe, tense, or uncomfortable.
- You feel a sense of being trapped or attacked.
- You feel bad vibes. You can't wait to get away from them.

Words can hurt

Let's start with the saying "Sticks and stones may break my bones, but words will never hurt me." This is used when a person is defending himself against another person who is using negative words to hurt the person. But is this the case?

No, actually words can truly hurt, and hearing them can lead to more stress! This is not referring to constructive criticism, which can be helpful and help you correct how you are doing something, but to such things as lies, rumors, and bullying.

Let's consider the life of an unpopular teenager who is bullied at school. The life of this person is filled with suffering and anxiety, which is a result of being picked on. The bullies may spread lies and rumors to others to intensify things.

This type of thing doesn't only happen to teens. Negative people in our adult lives can go behind our backs and spread lies and rumors. But we have to come to a realization that we have to confront these people and tell them know how we feel. Let your voice be heard. Your intellect will overcome negativity. If you cannot reason with these people, you must ultimately let them go.

What hurts the most is when we find out that it's people we know who are the ones hurting us. This only increases stress and depression. It is true to that one should try to "be the bigger person," ignoring what people say, ignoring negative people, and moving on, but at the end of the day, these behaviors can lower our self-esteem and make us depressed. Some negative words often go deeper into our souls. When lies are being circulated about someone, they can lead to various other problems as well. The sad thing is that many of us don't know what to do.

It is crucial that we wake up, take these problems seriously, and let our voices be heard. Many people are dying daily as a result of this, and many people are getting mentally sick. We cannot just ignore this any longer. We have to take a stand against these behaviors and get back to a healthy and happy environment.

Keep pictures around that make you happy

We've all heard that a picture is worth a thousand words. We could also say that a picture can bring thousands of feelings. When we look at old pictures, they bring back many memories—of people who have moved away, people who have passed away, or just happy memories in general. It is important to have your pictures available for viewing when you are stressed or in a bad mood. You might even consider enlarging some of your pictures and hanging them have around your home or office.

You can also compile anything that will make you feel better about yourself—awards, notes from others, or inspirational quotes—and put them together in a large photo frame or into a scrapbook. Put it in a place where you will be exposed to it on a daily basis, like in the bedroom, living room, kitchen, or your office. This can inspire you to love yourself more, especially on bad days when you need it the most. This can also help your relationship with your spouse or significant other. Keep a separate scrapbook or photo frame for your relationship with your partner. You can use it when you need a pick-me-up or when the two of you are going through a rough time. In addition, this guide will make you love yourself much more.

Guide 8: Loving yourself more

1. Find out what you're not happy with

Identify what makes you unhappy. It is great to make a list of your positive traits, but making a list about what you don't like is useful as well. However, don't stop there. Instead of just writing down what you want to replace, write down in detail how exactly you're going to replace it.

There are so many ways to improve on things you don't like, including taking classes, working out, meeting new people, learning new skills, or finding a new job. The important thing is to focus on changing things for the better and feeling good because of them, not focusing on the negative.

2. Do more for yourself

So many daily activities are about doing things for others or taking care of things that have to be done, such as taking the kids to school, grocery shopping, paying the bills . . . Stop being busy and think about when was the last time you did something for yourself. If it has been awhile, you need to take more personal time. It's not going necessarily make you love yourself more, but it certainly helps. Some options to consider include getting a massage, watching your favorite movie, buying yourself a present, spending a few hours reading a book, or eating your favorite dessert once a week.

If you rarely do anything for yourself, you should make sure to take more personal time and not feel guilty about it. It's amazing how many of us only spend 5 percent of the week on ourselves and still feel guilty. Instead, this should make us feel rejuvenated afterward, which will help us put more positive energy toward other areas of out lives. Take time for yourself. You're important, and you deserve it. Be proud and confident.

Helpful tip: Make your birthday into your own holiday. Make that day all about you. Invite your friends and loved one to enjoy your day with you. Go out and have fun—or treat and pamper yourself at home.

3. Forgive yourself

This is one of the most difficult things for people to deal with. As humans, we all make mistakes. Once we do, we should deal with them accordingly and tell ourselves that we shouldn't worry much about this one mistake but instead learn our lesson and not do it again. This will makes a huge, positive difference.

Forgiving yourself for your mistakes is one of the most important ways to learn to love yourself. This doesn't just mean forgiving the mistakes from your past, but also learning that it's okay to forgive yourself for any you may make in the future. Everyone makes mistake, and no one is perfect. The key is to learn from your mistakes and do everything in your power not to make the same ones again.

4. Start fresh each day

Start every day as if it's a fresh beginning, which it truly is. After forgiving yourself, concentrate on today. Love yourself and improve your life.

Spending some time focusing on yourself isn't selfish. You may not realize it, but when you truly love yourself, all that love and positive feeling can transfer to those around you as well as to other areas of your life. You will feel happy to help others. Don't think this will happen overnight, but don't give up on yourself either. The more you work on it, the more likely it is to happen. Here are some ideas:

- Find something about yourself that you like. It doesn't matter what it is—it just has to be something positive. It doesn't have to be something positive physically. Doing something good at work, a favor for a friend, and handling a difficult situation well all count as something positive. Again, use these positive things to replace the negative.

- Treat yourself when you come up with something positive about yourself.

Develop a positive attitude in yourself. Continue to reinforce this positive thinking. We have to make our positive thoughts more powerful than negative thoughts. So create a new way of thinking about yourself. If necessary, repeat it over and over until you find something positive about yourself and reinforce it when negative thoughts try to go come back.

Helpful tip: You could get together with a support group once a week. With friends and family, it's as if you are attending a "happy place workshop" once a week (or as many times as you want), sharing your feelings and enjoying the comfort and support.

CHAPTER 7

You Do Make a Difference

Thousands of candles can be lighted from a single candle, and the life of the candle will not be shortened. Happiness never decreases by being shared.

—Buddha

If you can't feed a hundred people, then feed just one.

—Mother Teresa

Answer this question honestly: do you really think you can make a difference in the world? Most of us would answer no, not believing that we have what it takes to make a difference to the world. We believe that only people like Mahatma Gandhi, Mother Teresa, Dr. Martin Luther King, and Albert Einstein can make a difference.

In actuality, every one of us is in this world to contribute and make a difference, one way or another. It does not have to be anything too big. It could be as simple as planting a tree. We have to believe in ourselves. Keep this in mind: we come to this world, we will leave this world, but stays are the memories. We are all capable of doing something good; it just comes down to our intentions. We have good and bad intensions.

Having good intentions is basically having the intention of doing something good, contributing or helping others in a time of need. By doing good, we feel a sense of overwhelming happiness, thus leading us to our happy place.

Bad intentions are exactly the opposite and may include harming others for one's selfish benefits. With bad intentions, a person may have many negative feelings, such as greed, lust, and envy, and the person is always unsatisfied with what he has.

How can we have good intentions? There is a way to go about doing good. The following is a guide to how people like us can make a difference in the world. We should use our time more productively by doing activities that matter. When it comes to making a difference, nothing matters more than taking action.

Guide 9: Making a difference one step at a time

1. Praise people more often

You can make a difference by helping one person at a time. One of the ways to help someone is to empower him. But how do you empower a person? Well, one of the ways is to be generous in giving praise and encouragement instead of criticism.

Praising someone for something is crucial. It is one of the most powerful communication tools. You are always in an environment to praise someone; it could be at your workplace, with your family or friends, or even at a ball game. When you praise someone, it will make a huge difference in that person's life.

By praising and encouraging others, we help them accomplish what they are meant to be, and that leads to more value being added to the world. Praising others can raise their confidence and their performance. It can make everyone's day better.

It is important to praise someone by starting with his name. By saying his name, it shows you notice and respect the person, just as you likely feel that way when someone knows your name. Most important, be specific when praising him. Instead of just saying, "Good job," you can say, "I was impressed with your work on putting up all the decorations for the party in time."

Always praise someone honestly. Don't play with emotions or give false praise. Think about when you were praised because of something good you'd done. You valued the praise because you valued the person's opinion and trusted the sincerity of the person giving it.

2. Volunteering

One of the biggest ways to make a difference is by volunteering. When we look at all the problems in the world, we might feel intimidated and wonder how one person really can make a difference—and what's the point?

Think about it this way: Suppose you want to move a heavy object. You, as one person, can push it, but it might move less than an inch. Then people slowly join you, until the object is moved to the final destination. Volunteering is the same way. It starts with one person. Then, if everyone as a whole comes together to work on the same problem, they can make it better, or even make it go away. Every person is important, and every person can do some good.

Now that you know you can make a difference by volunteering, what kind of volunteering should you do? Think about what you're into. What are you passionate about? What's out there in the world that catches your interest? What do you want to do in the near future? The answers to these questions will help point you to where you can volunteer for a cause or a group you'd like being part of. For instance:

- If you've always loved animals, you can volunteer to care for abandoned pets at an animal shelter.
- If you like to help people after a natural disaster, you can look for a Red Cross volunteer program in your local area or go to the Internet to find other options.
- If you like organizing things, you can become a fund-raiser for a charity, such as for those suffering in Bangladesh or East Africa. Go online or to a local charity office to see how you can help.

You can make a difference by doing little things, such as giving your old coat to a homeless person or planting a tree in your neighborhood. Sometimes there are things that need improving or people who need help, but we can't see them by just looking around. Try religious places, schools, and community centers to ask about volunteering and about worthy causes with which you can get involved. Again, there are websites that can match you up with projects that interest you.

3. Be a role model

Many of us may think that in order to become a role model, one must be famous or be an exceptional athlete like Michael Jordan. But in actuality, if you want to be a role model, you don't have to be famous or athletic.

A role model is someone we admire, respect, or simply look up to. We look for someone who is doing what we want to do in a way that we can emulate, or at least want to follow, and consider that person as an example of what we want to be. We could also call them our heroes. Many of us have athletes, teachers, parents, or mentors as role models.

Again, we too can be role models for someone. When we lead by positive example and have a positive life, someone will always want to follow and lead by those examples. For instance, if one of your teachers helps you during a difficult studying time, that will motivate you to help another student. Through example, it is up to you to meet their expectations and show them the right from the wrong way. It's a rewarding feeling to be a good role model and have the leadership skills to help others follow your example.

- You can be a Big Brother or Big Sister. Check online or go to your local church, school, or any other organization.
- Be an inspiration. Always do what you do best. It doesn't matter whether you're a parent, teacher, athlete, or a writer. You may not notice that there are people or kids learning from what you do.

4. Simple tasks make a big difference

We can do so many simple things to make a difference. It doesn't have to be anything out of this world. If you want to feed the poor, you don't have to feed one hundred people at once. Start with one person. You already have what it takes to make the world a better place. Making a difference to the world may seem like an enormous task, but it starts with one person, in fact. It's not the size of the contribution that matters most—it's having the heart to do it.

Thus we need do it today. Not this week, not tomorrow. Start today. There isn't any better time to start making a difference in the world. You don't need to wait until you have the time to share some love; you don't have to wait until you make more money to share some food. You can start making small contributions today and make a huge difference.

Contribute as much as you can. Keep in mind that your contribution is never too small, and it will make a difference. Can you imagine if everyone started to think the same way—how much of a difference we could make? Go online and find out how you can contribute to people in need, remembering always that you don't have to be concerned about whether it's a large or small contribution. What counts is the effort.

> *Do a good deed. If not for others, do it for*
> *the sake of yourself.*
>
> —Frasier

Love, happiness, and knowledge are the greatest gifts of all

Happiness and love are the two greatest gifts you can give someone. Too often, we are too much into ourselves and forget there are people in this world whom we can make feel a little happier and more loved.

As the saying goes, "To receive, you must first give." The more you give, the more you'll receive. Let us remind ourselves that in order to receive more happiness and love, we need to spread more of them first. It is contagious.

Give the gift of wisdom and see the long-lasting effects. As the saying goes, "Give a man a fish; you feed him for a day. Teach him how to fish; you feed him for a lifetime." It's good to do things that will make a difference, but when we make a difference, we should focus on the long-lasting effect rather than a temporary effect. For example, if we make contributions to build a school, it will benefit many people for years to come. And more people receiving education means more professionals contributing to the world.

One way we can make a difference is by influencing others to start doing things that make a difference. And the best way to influence others is to lead by example. Here are some suggestions:

- Start doing whatever is within your ability today.
- Start showing more concern and love to the people around you.
- Start donating monthly to your favorite charity.
- Start putting more effort in your work to increase the out put value
- Every effort counts, no matter how small and insignificant it may seem. Just do something . . . and do something good.

CHAPTER 8

The Power of Optimism

When you are asked if you can do a job, tell 'em, "Certainly I can!" Then get busy and find out how to do it.

—Theodore Roosevelt

Optimism comes from the Latin word "optimus," meaning "best," which describes an optimistic person who is always looking for the best in any situation and expecting good things to happen. Optimism is a belief, expecting or hoping that things will turn out well and for the best. Even if something bad happens, the result will be good.

Psychology studies show that an optimist has better mental and physical health. Research also suggests that optimists have a long list of social benefits over the pessimist. Optimists live longer, they recover from illness at a greater rate, and they have more productive and longer-lasting relationships.

Optimism and pessimism are not innate

We are not born optimistic or pessimistic. We learn both qualities. Both may very well date to our early years in life, shaping our attitudes toward later events in life.

Being an optimist or a pessimist boils down to the way you think of yourself and your actions.

- Optimists believe that their actions can result in positive things happening. They feel that they are responsible for their own happiness, and that they can expect more good things to happen in the future.
- Optimists don't blame themselves when bad things happen. They view bad events as results of something outside of themselves.
- An optimistic person would see losing his job as an opportunity, perhaps to start his own business or invest his money. (Your severance)
- An optimist sees the best-case scenario in many situations.

However, a pessimist thinks the opposite way. He blames himself for the bad things that happen in his life and thinks that one mistake means more will come.

It comes down to the way we think, or our thought processes, and how we think things will turn out. Optimists believe they have a much brighter future. Optimists view a bad situation or unexpected event as a temporary setback, not a permanent one. Even if something bad happens today, optimists believe that good things will come again in the future. As with the loss of a job, an optimist sees the brighter side. For many of us, getting fired or laid off from a job can be difficult and frustrating, often making us feel a sense of failure, but an optimist will view this as an opportunity to go back to school, start his own business, or explore other possibilities. Optimistic people would say that losing their job was the push they needed.

Optimists are also good at helping others see the "brighter side" and other possibilities. They help people see the unseen benefits and creative solutions. As with kindness and happiness, their attitude can be contagious.

Being an optimist does not mean being ignorant and having blind faith, which can lead a person to make a wrong decision or be impractical. An optimist is always realistic, acknowledging obstacles and challenges, but is not easily discouraged by stress or unexpected circumstances.

Guide 10: How can one become an optimist?

You can be an optimist. These other positive characteristics that many optimists share increase overall happiness and promote health while reducing stress and anxiety:

- Think about the good things in life and emphasize them more.
- Be grateful and thankful for your all your blessings.
- Don't complain when bad things happen. Embrace them.
- Have courage in feeling that nothing can hold you back from achieving success and reaching your goals.
- Be confident that the world offers plenty of opportunities for you to succeed.

It's simple—once you change the way you think, you can change your life. The good news is that you can change your thought processes. With enough practice, even a pessimist can become an optimist. All you need to do is to change how you think, and how you think something will happen. Instead of thinking that something negative will happen, reevaluate the situation and figure out what positive can come of it.

Let's say you failed an exam at school. Think about what you learned during the process. Did you need more study time or less distraction, or was it nervousness? Figure out what strengths you discovered within yourself, and when you take your exam again, you will do better. Virtually any failure can be turned into a learning experience, which increases your potential for success in the future.

Optimism is a quality in achieving success and having a positive outlook

Optimism is a quality that will give you an advantage in getting a better career and being successful in life. Life is too short to be upset and frustrated, so start turning your thinking around to positive thoughts and an optimistic outlook. Overall happiness can advance your career, relationships, and other part of your life.

Many of us have heard this question: "Is the glass half-full or half-empty?" Answering this question comes down to how you look at life—through either optimistic eyes or pessimistic eyes.

When you think of the word optimism, perhaps you think of happy, smiling, and joyous people. But in reality, optimism does not mean that you don't have any worries and are constantly happy; it simply means that you have a positive outlook on life. It means that that you appreciate and value hope. An optimistic person will always hope for the best and prepare for the worst.

One of the most important traits of an optimist is perseverance. The person stays at a steady course of action, working hard and being persistent. Optimists will last through tough times. They have enough faith in their abilities and enough self-esteem to carry them through rough times, even if the situation lasts for a while. Optimists believe that their actions matters. They do not complain about what needs to be changed in the world, but they do believe they matter in the world. Optimism is all about an outlook. It is less about how you are being treated and more about how you can treat others.

> *Even if I knew that tomorrow the world would*
> *go to pieces, I would still plant my apple tree.*
> —Martin Luther

Optimistic people tend to pay closer attention to their health issues than pessimists do. They don't blame themselves for everything. They work through setbacks more effectively and are better able to eliminate negative people, events, and situations from their lives.

Exercise

- Write down short statements that will remind you to want positive things to happen in your life or the world. Put them in places where you will see them on a regular basis or keep them in your wallet or pocket at all times for quick reference.

- Stay focused on the list. If you set your focus, it is where your life is going to be headed. Focusing on the positive aspects and the solutions in your life will eventually overtake the negativity and the problems. It doesn't mean your life will be a piece of cake, but you'll have the ability to recover more rapidly from temporary setbacks and steer life more effectively.

Harmony

Harmony is essentially an agreement feelings and opinion: to live in harmony. Harmony is the result of your mind-set, your actions, your thoughts, your experiences, your education, your goals, and your work all coming together in one space and time. Harmony is also a result of what you have done in the past opening the door to a good future. Yes, it involves the way that you think and the attitude you have about your possibilities in the world. Harmony is the result of optimism.

Optimism is not the antidote for world peace or for curing illness or ending hunger. But optimism is a step forward. Optimists are better able to cope with world issues. They are able to take failures and setbacks and not let them ruin their lives or self-esteem. Optimists are better able to accept and grow from constructive criticism. They take the advice and see it for what's worth and for how it may help them live better and more effectively.

Optimism is the first defense to challenge

Many people put optimism as the first defense and get good results on any challenges that life can bring about. Optimists are people who have the most options. They look at a challenge and are not put down by it because they belief that it will change and it is not going last forever.

Optimists seem to be more creative and work harder for positive outcomes. They are not afraid of what they do not know or what lies ahead. They are levelheaded about most events and are usually not discouraged about resolving them.

If you want to be optimistic, you have to make conscious and effective choices on a daily basis, as this is not a one-time act. If you want to be optimistic in life, you need to continue to examine the challenges you encounter on a daily basis and choose to look at the positives rather than the negatives. In other words, you have to start seeing the glass as half-full, not half-empty. The positive belief that you will succeed will increase your chances of achieving a successful outcome. Start each day with a positive outlook on life.

CHAPTER 9

Morals/The Big Push

Moral excellence comes about as a result of habit. We become just by doing just acts, temperate by doing temperate acts, brave by doing brave acts.

—Aristotle

Like religion, morals (and morality) are complex. Let's simplify it. We may look at morals as simply being what is right or wrong. When we are faced with moral questions in our daily lives, just as when we are faced with many different issues, sometimes we act impulsively or instinctively, and sometimes we have to make a decision as to what we should do.

Research shows that a person who possesses traits such as good moral values makes better decisions about any situation. A moral person is typically happier, and people are more likely to follow and listen to someone who has high spirits. Thus we can look at a good, moral person as someone who is confident in himself.

Every one of us needs a moral push occasionally. As you look back on your life, you can probably remember times when you needed a push to overcome a new challenge or stress. Thankfully, many of us had people in our lives who enthusiastically provided that push when we needed it most. Some of us even now have family, friends, or colleagues who give us that extra boost.

We can revisit those important moments of our lives that required us to get a push or provide a push for someone else. We have all found some things both difficult and challenging and actually questioned whether they were the right thing to do at the time, but we were fortunate that most of the decisions were correct—like making the decision to attend college, for example. Many of may think a lot and may not attend college, but we have those special people who gave us the push to go. Making our futures better.

Looking at the lives of many influential people who became leaders, we see that they had to work hard to overcome many obstacle and rejections before they became leaders. Many of them become leaders because of the support and extra boost as well as the ability to go forward with the push of their families, friends, and supporters to promote peace, change lives, and make people understand their teachings of unity.

As people, we will never outgrow the need for a good moral push. There will always be a need to tackle new challenges in the pursuit of success and happiness. So whether you need a moral boost or need to give a moral boost, keep an open mind and be ready. You will be surprised to see the difference it makes.

Good people have good morals

It is known that a person who has high morals is able to deal with challenges more successfully and is not easily discouraged. A moral person is effective and better at handling unexpected events and making good judgments. This person is able to express his opinions and thoughts quickly, allowing him to give good advice or a moral push. We should all want to strive to be a good person.

Even people who are doing bad things may think they are actually doing good. Knowing what is good and what is bad can be difficult since there are so many bad temptations. Everyone has a good side and a bad side, and knowing the difference between good and bad is a start in the right direction. Having good morals and sticking to them can make you a good person.

What are good morals?

We believe that a moral person is a good person who helps and does the best as far as others are concerned. For instance, we all know this universal rule: "Do unto others as you would have them do unto you." The next time you help someone in need, it will eventually come back to you. Some of us believe people who follow the rules are moral or good, as rules are believed to be there so people do not get hurt or hurt other people, creating a balance in our society.

A good, moral person takes care of and helps those in need, whether family, friends, neighbors, or even enemies. That's right. Caring for people you don't like can be hard, but you will find it rewarding if you put your differences aside. You will be a good person for doing so. Again, love yourself first. If you do not love yourself, then it will be hard to love others.

Being good—it's in our minds

You can choose to be good. Choosing between right and wrong will help us become better people. As we are aware, everyone has his own understanding of right and wrong, good and bad. But all of us should agree that as long as we don't cause harm, have conflicts, or stand in the way of someone, we are on the right track to being a good, moral person. Staying positive and happiness can make you a good person and bring you closer to your happy place.

If you believe that you can be good, then you will be a good person. Being happy makes you a good person because happiness is contagious, causing others to be happy. Smile, smile, and smile! Choose to be happy.

In our society, we blame, judge, and criticize other people. We should all be aware of how we think about others. Keep an open mind and always try to think the best about others. Don't assume the worst. Contributing your time and energy to helping others can help you become a good person. Help others as much as you can, because there are other people who are worse off than you are. For example, if you know someone taking on a big task or a promotion, you can offer your advice. If you know someone who has had a death in the family, you can offer your time and comfort.

CHAPTER 10

Practical Solutions and Final Thoughts

In the end we are all separate: our stories, no matter how similar, come to a fork and diverge. We are drawn to each other because of our similarities, but it is our differences we must learn to respect.

Unknown

Live simply

We live in a complex society. Our lives are busy: we rush into tasks, and we try to finish them in one day or in a short period. Rushing from one place to the next, we miss out on all the scenery and don't realize until the end of day that we are exhausted and stressed out from all the chaos of the day. We have to realize that we need to take time for what really should be important to us, what we really want to be doing, like spending time with loved ones and doing things we're passionate about.

It is important to understand that life doesn't have to be like that. Live your life simpler, in a place where stress, circumstances, and chaos don't take over. Most important, decide what is important to you. Is it your job? Your busy schedule? Or is it spending time with your loved ones and friends or accomplishing a goal?

It is important to make a day less busy. It's good to have a plan or a to-do list, but don't fill it up too much. This will lead to rushing, and when you rush to do a task, it often fails. Take time out to spend quality time with loved ones and do breathing techniques and stretching at least once a day.

Live your life as simply as possible. Minimize your expenses. When shopping, only buy things that are necessary and that will be important to you. Get up and walk more often. Go to the park or the garden, get some fresh air, smell the flowers, and be one with nature. Get some sun exposure. In many studies, sunlight has been shown to put people in a better mood.

Find natural solutions when it comes to stress and illness. This may be the solution for maintaining your health and vitality. Live life as simply as possible, for it will be most rewarding.

Final thoughts

"Your outlook on life is a direct reflection of how much you like yourself."

We should all find and maintain a happy place. Not all of us are able to do so, but some people are definitely better getting theirs than others are. Studies on what makes people find their happy place revealed that it doesn't have much to do with material goods or success; in actuality, it seems to depend on your outlook on life, the quality of your relationships with the people around you, and your connection with nature.

As we know, an optimistic person is one who looks on the brighter sides of things or takes hopeful views about life situations. Being an optimist, you will trust and anticipate that life will turn out to be the best it can, and you look forward to the future with a smile.

However, being an optimist does not mean that you should be out of touch with reality or ignore obligations and obstacles in life and behave in an irrational manner. Also, it does not mean waiting for things to happen automatically. It means expecting the best, believing that the best will happen to you—but at the same time, making the right decisions to make it happen, following your decisions, and acting appropriately in realizing them.

- An optimist sees an opportunity in every difficulty.
- An optimist can differentiate good from bad, but at the same time expects success in all his endeavors and acts in a proactive manner to make things turn out well. The optimistic person is motivated and energetic, pursuing his desires with confidence and happiness.

So while you may read or participate in activities to help go to your happy place, the main thing that will help boost your happiness is improving your attitude toward life.

Always believe in yourself and follow your instincts. For instance, the next time you go shopping, look at two shirts. With one shirt, analyze your decision carefully, weighing the pros and cons, and with the other, listen to your gut. Studies show that the shirt you buy when following your gut will make you happier than the one you analyzed.

Now, some of our decisions are more important than picking out shirts, but by the time you're looking over your choice, the options you're weighing are probably similar, and the difference will only temporarily affect your happiness. So the next time you have a decision to make and you're down to two or three options, just pick the one that feels right and go with it. Never regret the decisions you make.

Money isn't everything, but it sure does help. When we are asked what is wrong, some of us answer, "I have money problems." In our society, we are led to believe that we need material goods to be happy and we need to buy what everyone else has, but we need to realize the value of hard-earned money and spend accordingly. Too much spending leads to one of life's main problems: debt. Don't go under pressure. Believe in your decisions as to how to spend your money, mainly on the important things such as food, shelter, and clothing.

"What if I don't make enough money?" you may be asking. According to statistics, a person who makes forty thousand dollars a year in the United States will meet his financial needs, considering where one lives. Are you making enough? If not, examine the reason. Many of us are capable of doing so much more. Perhaps you will decide to get training to secure a better job or try to move up in the company. Or maybe you will choose to explore other options—things you are passionate about—perhaps singing, writing, or photography.

One thing you have in common with a millionaire is time. We are all given 24 hours a day, 7 days a week, and 365 days a year. Make use of the time that you have.

So does that mean that any money you make beyond the statistics will make you happier? Not necessarily. Don't get me wrong—money makes a difference in how much you can purchase, and if you think making more money will make you more happier, maybe it will, but statistically it probably won't. Once you make enough money to support your basic needs, the level of happiness will not likely be affected by how much money you make, and it will not improve the relationships you have with people.

Your comfort may increase with more money, but comfort is only temporary. Some may say it is an "illusion," taking our minds off what matters the most in life. Studies also show that being comfortable makes people want more and more. Making more money usually leads to more expenses and then to more problems. Or it creates greed. That's why it's important to push beyond your comfort zone and focus on your personal growth and improving relationships with others.

Be close to your family and friends. Don't allow yourself to be socially distant. In our society, we tend to be apart from our love ones. If possible, move to where your family is so you can see them more and have a better social connection. We are always on the move. We take jobs across the country and sometimes across the world so we can make more money. Or we have a conflict and move way. The fact is that our relationships with our friends and family have a far greater impact on our happiness than our jobs or misunderstandings do.

Think about it this way: "Money costs too much." It can distance us from things we care about. The relationships we share with our loved ones are worth more than any amount of wealth in the world. We could even say that they are priceless. So have more connection with one another and communicate more often.

Find a happy place in where you are now. Many of us expect that the right job and a healthy relationship will get us dramatically closer to our happy place, but research makes it clear that if you have a positive outlook, you will make the best of any situation, and if you have good relationships with people, you won't depend on your setbacks to give your life a greater sense of meaning. You'll find it in your closeness with the people you care about.

That doesn't mean that you shouldn't work toward a job that will make you happier; it means you should understand that the amount of happiness from your job or money is quite small when compared to your outlook on life and your relationships with people.

Laugh more often. Psychologists agree that laughter is the best medicine, so laugh often, and whether you feel happy or not, your mood will change. Smile more often and watch a lot of situations change.

Practice forgiveness. Studies show that the attitude of forgiveness gives you a better lifestyle and better health. You could say that forgiveness literally heals your mind and body. Studies also suggest that it lowers stress. Try to forgive and forget. Don't let your anger get the best of you.

Understand yourself. See if you can find interest in faith and spirituality. People with faith and spirituality tend to provide more support when we are in need of help. They can strengthen others, give social support, offer firm beliefs, and help people resolve and heal many issues. They can also restore us to faith, oftentimes making us open to caring and loving. If religious activities are not your thing, you can look some other place to find friends who have the same mutual interests as you.

Writing space

Look at the list from chapter 1, things we think will make us go to our happy place. Examine the list and carefully choose the things that make you go to your happy place. Choose the things that will help you go beyond your stress and comfort zone to achieve self-improvement and personal growth. Be honest and open. Commit fully.

BIBLIOGRAPHY

Bauer, Joy, MS, RD, CDN, *Food Cures: Treat Common Health Concerns, Look Younger, and Live Longer* (2007).

Ben-Shahar, Tal, PhD, *Happier: Learn the secrets to daily joy and lasting fulfillment* (2002).

Benson, Herbert, MD, *The Relaxation Response* (1974).

Canfield, Jack, Mark Victor Hanson, and Ann Newark, Forward by Debrah Noville, *Chicken Soup for the Soul. Think Positive: 101 Inspirational Stories about Counting Your Blessings and Having a Positive Attitude* (2010).

George, Mike, *Learn to Relax: A Practical Guide to Easing Tension and Conquering Stress* (1998).

Jenner, Paul, *How to Be Happier* (2007, 2010).

McKenna, Paul, *I Can Make You Confident: The Power to Go for Anything You Want!* (2010).

Nepo, Mark, *Finding Inner Courage* (2007).

Orloff, Judith, MD, *Positive Energy: 10 Extraordinary Prescriptions for Transforming Fatigue, Stress and Fear into Vibrance, Strength and Love* (2004, 2005).

Seligman, Martin E.P., PhD, *Learned Optimism: How to Change Your Mind and Your Life* (1990).

Sivanada Yoga Vedanta Centre, *Yoga Mind and Body* (1996, 2008).

Smith, Ian K., MD, *Happy: Simple Steps for Getting the Life You Want* (2010).

Spadaro, Patricia, *Honor Yourself: The Inner Art of Giving and Receiving* (2009).

Sparks, Susan, Rev., *Laugh Your Way to Grace: Reclaiming the Spiritual Power of Humor* (2010, 2011).

Stoddard, Alexandra, *Choosing Happiness: Keys to a Joyful Life* (2002).

Urban, Hal, *Positive Words, Powerful Results. Simple Ways to Honor, Affirm, and Celebrate Life* (2004).

Internet Sources

www.urbandictionary.com

www.helpguide.org

www.answers.com

www.stressreductionbasics.com

www.wikihow.com

www.howstuffworks.com

www.yoga-about.com

www.volunteermatch.org

http://www.answers.com/topic/moral-
    example#ixzz1VjxpYVBb

www.ezinearticles.com

ACKNOWLEDGMENTS

As I conducted research for this book, it was a therapeutic process, but there is so much more that goes into this topic than you can find on the pages of any book. I urge people to use all the resources in the world to find peace of mind.

With that being said, I would like to thank the positive people around me, such as my family and friends, especially my family, who gave me inspiration, desire, and ambition to find my place in life and share my ideas on the pages of this book. I would also like to thank all the great authors who write motivational, self-help, and self-improvement books. Without these references, I wouldn't be able to find my place and share with everyone.

All of us have a purpose. We are all given an opportunity to do something. I would like to urge everyone to believe in yourself and find what makes you go forward. That is the key to finding your *happy place*.